Bibliographic information published by the German National Library:

The German National Library lists this publication in the National Bibliography; detailed bibliographic data are available on the Internet at http://dnb.dnb.de .

Imprint:

Copyright © 2005 GRIN Verlag, Open Publishing GmbH
Print and binding: Books on Demand GmbH, Norderstedt Germany
ISBN: 978-3-640-11438-2

This book at GRIN:

http://www.grin.com/en/e-book/110003/the-jdo-persistence-model

Stefan Marr

The JDO Persistence Model

GRIN Publishing

GRIN - Your knowledge has value

Since its foundation in 1998, GRIN has specialized in publishing academic texts by students, college teachers and other academics as e-book and printed book. The website www.grin.com is an ideal platform for presenting term papers, final papers, scientific essays, dissertations and specialist books.

Visit us on the internet:

http://www.grin.com/

http://www.facebook.com/grincom

http://www.twitter.com/grin_com

The JDO Persistence Model

by

Stefan Marr

The Java Data Objects Persistence Model

Stefan Marr

Seminar System Modeling 2005
Hasso-Plattner-Institute for Software Systems Engineering

stefan.marr@hpi.uni-potsdam.de

Abstract

JDO is a specification for design object domain models without having to consider the persistency of data. The main target of JDO is the abstraction of concrete data storage solutions and the provision of transparent and implementation-independent solutions for persistent data.

Starting with an introduction to the architectural model of Java Data Objects, benefits of this approach and the realization by a tool-based enhancement are outlined. Furthermore, the API itself is in focus of examination, main programming interfaces and the JDO-QL will be discussed.

Finally, it is aimed to give an outlook on the upcoming JDO 2.0 specification.

Keywords: Java, Persistence, JDO, Database, Code Enhancement

1. Introduction

Persistence of data is one of the main requirements of business application software. Relational databases are the most commonly used systems to meet these requirements. They are wide spread and highly optimized for performance and reliability. However, the use of RDBMS requires mapping of business object models to a specific database schema and introduces complexity and dependencies into the development process and the resulting product. This leads to a reduced exchangeability of the used data storage which delimitates the reusability and spectrum of applications.

So, an effort should be the introduction of a standardized abstraction layer. This entails independence of a specific data storage type, disposes the necessity of mapping your object model on a data schema, and reduces the modeling and programming complexity for persistence itself.

2. JDO

2.1. What is JDO?

The Java Data Objects (JDO) API is a standard interface-based definition of object persistence. It describes the transparent storage and retrieval of Java objects.

JDO is intended to provide transparent mechanisms to persist the whole object domain model of an application, including mapping of JDO instances to data storage and implicit updates of persistent object states.

It is intended to reduce most efforts of introducing a persistence layer by the use of automated enhancements.

Figure 1 is a simplified example of a typical application using JDO as persistence service. The [JDOSPEC] requires all JDO implementations to be binary compatible. Thereby, it is possible to exchange a specific JDO implementation and start to use another type of datastore without the need to recompile the whole application.

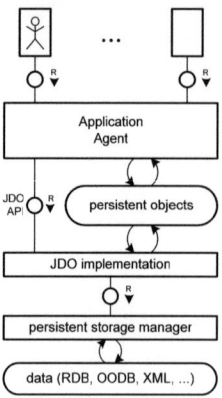

Figure 1 Structure of a JDO-based application

A JDO implementation, delivered by a third-party vendor is highly optimized on a particular data storage system like common RDBMS, ODBMS, or maybe XML-based file storage depending on the area of application. The introduced abstraction layer results in an application

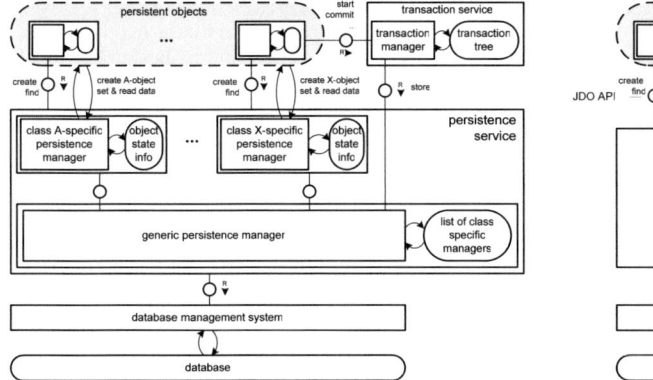

Figure 3.1 Persistence without and with JDO

Figure 3.2 Persistence with JDO

which is independent of a single data storage type and could be used with a variety of different kinds of these systems.

2.2. Advantages of using JDO

In Figure 2 a FMC based block diagram is intended to visualize the different modeling efforts. Figure 2.1 illustrates an application, which uses a relational database system for persistence and services implementing class specific persistence methods. Figure 2.2 displays an application using JDO for data persistence.

The system on the left hand side consists of a generic persistency manager which implements the main functionality and a number of class specific persistence managers which realize the data storage and retrieval for the class specific attributes based on a mapping between attributes and rows in a database schema. For each class in the object domain model a specific persistence manager is necessary. In addition, a *transaction service* has to be implemented which might be provided by a used persistence framework, but in general it is a service tailored to a specific *generic persistence manager*.

Figure 2.2 displays the Java Data Objects way. Most functionality is realized by the JDO implementation. The transaction service is part of the specification and class persistence is implemented by transparent techniques. There is no programming or modeling effort to get these functionalities. The operations like creating, finding, modifying, or storing persistent objects are covered by the JDO API. Initial operations like make

an object persistent or delete it from the data store are realized by the JDO *PersistenceManager* interface. A small introduction to the main interfaces is given in a later section of this paper.

This architecture results in a storage-type independent object model and provides access to persistent data objects without knowledge of internal mapping or data store specific query languages.

2.3. Environments for JDO

JDO is intended to be used in two types of environments, non-managed and managed environments.

In a non-managed environment the application is directly connect to resources it needs and it is responsible for invocation of persistence actions on objects or configuration of connections to resources. In such environments the programmer and application are independent of e.g. J2EE container technologies but have to handle all interactions with the underlying persistence service.

In contrast to this, managed environments like J2EE-based multi-tier applications provide, in conjunction with the used container, special mechanisms for declarative configuration of the persistence service in use.

Depending on the used container, the container itself takes responsibility for configuring the service, managing transactions, providing security services, or pooling of *PersistenceManagers*.

The JDO transactions are harmonized with J2EE transactions. It is up to the programmer to decide, which type of transaction will be used. JDO implementations can synchronize there transaction to distributed J2EE transactions. Standards like EJB, JSP, Servlets, CMT, and BMT are supported and JDO is designed to be used in such environments.

2.4. The Class Enhancement

The benefits in modeling and programming are achieved by an automated enhancement process. The JDO specification requires every JDO implementation to provide an enhancer tool, which is binary compatible to the standard. This enhancer tool will work on Java Bytecode files, the class files.

The structure and an example are shown in Figure 3. The developer will design a class according to domain requirements like an order for multiple items with a given date. This order should be persisted in a database with all associated items. Therefore, no changes have to be made on the domain model, neither by changes on attribute visibility nor by adding special persistence methods and attributes.

All necessary changes for realizing persistence will be added by the enhancer and do not influence the Java object model. The developer has to create an XML-file which names and describes the classes to be persisted. Depending on the used JDO implementation, there are several vendor-specific extensions to the XML-file possible. In some cases it is necessary to build a new application upon an existing database structure and the developer will have to map his class attributes on a database schema. Furthermore, the specification provides additional settings for persistent fields. It is possible to control the persistence behavior in more detail. Especially for collections and arrays handling and type of included objects has to be specified. In addition, the object identity type can be specified. For all unspecified details default settings are used.

After creating the JDO Metadata the developer can initiate the enhancement process. According to the named classes, the *JDO Enhancer* will modify the Java Bytecode. It will implement the *PersistenceCapable* interface and add several methods and fields to the classes. On the right side of

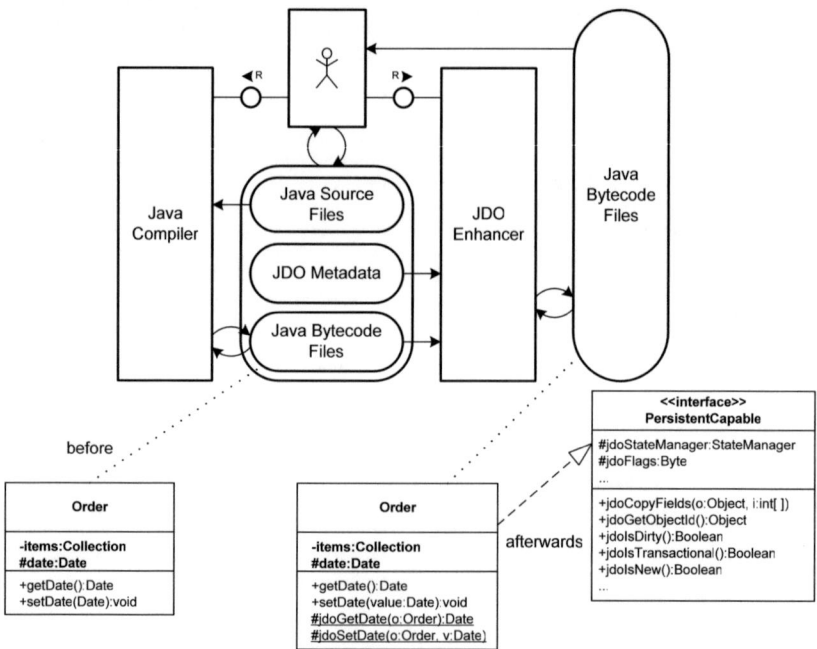

Figure 4 Enhancement and its effects

Figure 3 a couple of effects on data classes are outlined.

For each persistent attribute a set of getter and setter methods will be added and executable code, which accesses the attribute, will be changed to call the accessor or mutator methods. With these changes, the added *StateManager* is able to guarantee data persistence for all modifications on a single data object.

Even if it is possible to implement the *PersistenceCapable* interface manually it is strongly recommended not to do so. No methods and attributes with the prefix *jdo* should be used directly in unenhanced code. Most tasks can be done by using the JDOHelper class instead of calling these methods and attributes.

It is important to know that JDO Metadata will be used by the enhancer tool to identify classes to be made persistence capable, and some information like mapping rules or other vendor-specific enhancements are used at runtime. Therefore, behavior is not specified if the metadata is changed after initiating the enhancement process.

3. Using JDO

This part aims to give a short introduction into the main classes and interfaces a JDO programmer has to concern with. Furthermore, the used concepts for object identity, object lifecycle, and the JDO-Query Language are outlined. The relationships between main interfaces are illustrated in Figure 4.

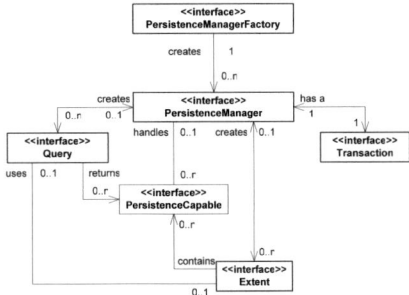

Figure 5 Main JDO Interfaces

3.1. The Persistence Manager

The main interface for application developers is the *PersistenceManager* interface. It is intended to be used for all persistence operations on *Persis-*

tenceCapable[1] objects and provides overloaded variants of most cache management and instance lifecycle methods. These methods manipulate single instances, collections, arrays of instances, or potentially all applicable instances in the cache. Besides, it is used to obtain *Query*, *Extent*, and *Transaction* objects.

Depending on the environment, there are several ways to retrieve such a manager object. In non-managed environments the concrete class *JDOHelper* makes the *PersistenceManagerFactory* available.

A *PersistenceManagerFactory* object is used to get an instance of *PersistenceManager*. Thereby, it is possible to get more than one *PersistenceManager* object from a single factory. The factory can even implement pooling.

In J2EE environments, it is possible to obtain a factory from properly configured JNDI (Java Naming and Directory Interface).

After obtaining a *PersistenceManager* object the following methods can be used by an application:

- *makePersistent(...)*
  These methods can be used to explicitly make transient objects persistent so they will be stored in the datastore after the transaction completes successfully. They can only be used within a transaction, otherwise a *JDOUserException* is thrown.
  In fact, applications rarely need to invoke *makePersistent()* directly. Usually, newly created objects are referenced by existing persistent objects, e.g. via a singleton reference or membership of a collection. In such cases, the new object will be transparently made persistent when the transaction is committed.

- *deletePersistent(...)*
  These methods delete persistent instances from the database and must be called in the context of an active transaction. The Java object thus remains, but no longer represents the persistent data store entity, which has been deleted. Unlike making objects persistent, deleting objects only deletes the specified instances. There is no reach-ability algorithm; referenced persistent objects are not deleted. To emulate this behavior, the *InstanceCallbacks* can be used to implement the *jdoPreDelete()* method to delete referred objects.

---
[1] In 2.4 the enhancement process is outlined which adds the *PersistenceCapable* interface to all class meant to be made persistent.

- *makeTransient(…)*
  Make a persistent instance transient again. This does not affect the underlying data store entity in any way. It does not delete the data. The instance will be disassociated from the datastore only, and any subsequent changes to the instance will not be synchronized with the datastore.
- *evict(…)* or *evictAll()*
  Evict the given or all cached persistence-capable instances from the cache.
  However, eviction is only a hint to the persistence manager that an instance should be removed from its cache. By default persisted objects are automatically evicted, and it is not necessary for an application to do it programmatically.
- *refresh(…)*
  These methods re-retrieve the values of the fields from the datastore for the specified instances, whether or not they have been already modified in the current transaction.

Furthermore, there are additional methods which will be discussed in more detail e.g. in [JDOAW2003] and [JDOPH2003].

3.2. Transactions

A transaction is a group of modifications on persistent objects; these modifications must be completed in its entirety or not at all. The demands for ACID (Atomic, Consistent, Isolated, Durable) have to be met.

Most resource managers allow different levels of isolation. Nevertheless, developers should not rely on any isolation level greater than Read Committed, because JDO does not explicitly specify the isolation level that will be applied.

On isolation level of Read Committed, state changes of persisted objects within a transaction cannot be seen by other transactions until a commit has been issued.

Per *PersistenceManager*, only a single transaction is possible at a time. Furthermore, JDO does not support the concept of nested transactions.

To work with concurrent transactions additional *PersistenceManager* instances are required, which may be provided by pooling via *PersistenceManagerFactory* or via methods in a J2EE environment.

JDO supports two transaction strategies. Pessimistic transactions are a required feature, whereas optimistic transactions are an optional feature.

Therefore, pessimistic transactions are the default. They are suitable for short-living transactions. Typically, there is no user interaction or other blocking operations between start and end of a transaction. This type of transaction will exclude other transactions from accessing data, which is accessed within.

When working with long-living transactions, it is often unacceptable to deny access on data used within this transaction, the complete period of time the transaction lasts. To reduce such data locking, optimistic transaction will not lock the accessed data. They may be implemented with native optimistic transactions of the underlying datastore or they are implemented using two pessimistic transactions.

The first pessimistic transaction is used to get the current state of used data objects from the data storage. This state will be saved for later data integrity checks.

After doing all modifications on the persistent objects over a longer period of time, the second pessimistic transaction is started. This one will retrieve the actual state from the datastore and compare it with the saved data. If the data integrity is ensured, all operations done on the data objects will be committed. If a concurrent operation has changed the data in the datastore, the whole optimistic transaction will fail and an exception will be thrown.

A transaction object can be obtained from the *PersistenceManager* by invocation of *currentTransaction()*. With *begin()* and *commit()* a demarcation of actions belonging to a transaction is done. *rollback()* is used to discard modifications on persistent objects in an erroneous transaction.

3.3. Object Identities

JDO provides three different kinds of identity for persisted objects. This is done to improve the transparency and the mechanisms provided by Java for identity (==) and equality (*equals()*) remain unaffected.

The default type of object identity is called Datastore Identity. A unique Identity is assigned to an object when it is made persistent. The nature of this Object-ID is handled internal by the JDO implementation and the underlying data store. Theoretically datastore identity corresponds to primary-keys in RDBS.

Application Identity is the second and most

complex type of object identity. It is used, if the object identity is derived from a subset of persistent fields of an object or created outside of the application, like ISBN.

For this type of identity, it is necessary to implement a specific Object-ID class, which fulfils special requirements. The Object-ID class has to implement the *java.io.Serializable* interface and the *toString()*, *equals()*, and *hashCode()* methods have to be overridden. All requirements are listed in section 5.4.1 of the [JDOSPEC].

The third, non-durable identity is used for objects without need for own identity, like simple lists or bulk data.

3.4. Object Lifecycle

JDO defines a number of states for persistent objects. These states are used by the JDO runtime to manage the in-memory lifecycle of persistent objects and to decide when data has to be synchronized with data store. Not all states are required by the specification. For instance *Persistent-Nontransactional*, Transient-Clean, and Transient-Dirty are optional states and are only required if a specific JDO implementation provides associated optional features.

In this section, only required states and state transitions are treated, which are also shown in Figure 5.

3.4.1. Transient

JDO does not influence standard object construction mechanisms in conjunction with the *new* operator. Therefore, all objects created with a developer-written constructor are transient by default. They behave like instances of the un-enhanced class. Until they are made persistent, there is no identity associated with these objects. Moreover, there is no handling of persistent fields and no transactional behavior.

If a transient object of an enhanced class is referred by a persistent object at commit time, it will be persisted.

3.4.2. Persistent-New

Instances are in this state if they have been made persistent during the current transaction. During the transition from transient to persistent, the associated *PersistenceManager* becomes responsible for handling further state transitions, handling of field values for rollbacks, and synchronization with data store. Furthermore, it will assign a JDO identity to the instance.

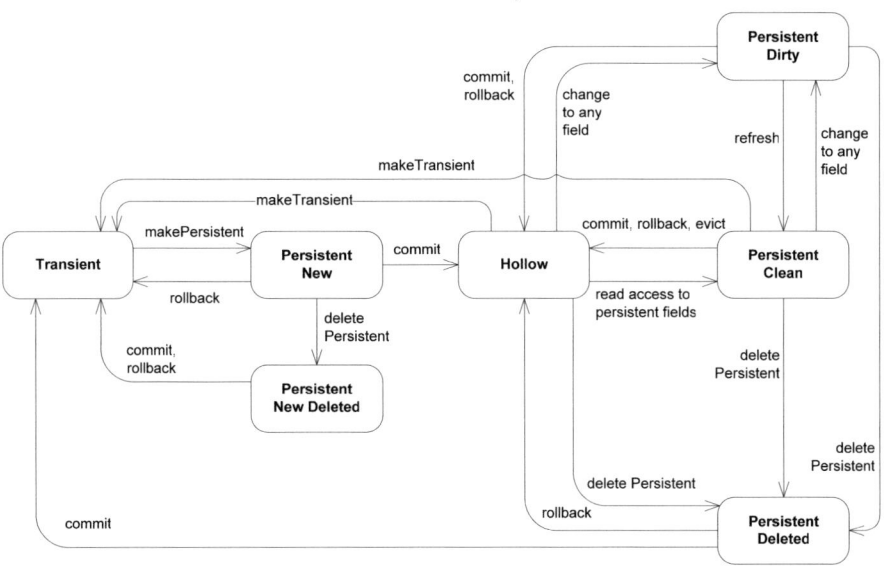

Figure 6 Object Lifecycle

3.4.3. Persistent-New-Deleted

This state will be reached if an object has made persistent and be deleted within one single transaction.

3.4.4. Hollow

Objects in the Hollow state are already persisted, but at this state only their object identity is loaded. All ordinary attribute values have not been loaded.

3.4.5. Persistent-Clean

The data of these objects had been read, but not modified within the current transaction.

3.4.6. Persistent-Dirty

The data of objects in this state had been changed in the current transaction, or the *makeDirty()* method of *JDOHelper* had been invoked.

A call to *makeDirty()* is useful, when changes to a persistent field of an array type had been made, since JDO does not require automatic tracking of changes made to array fields.

3.4.7. Persistent-Deleted

JDO instances that have been deleted in the current transaction are Persistent-Deleted.

3.5. Extents

An Extent represents the complete set of all persistent instances of a class. It is obtained from a *PersistenceManager* by *getExtent* and it is possible to decide whether items of subclasses should be included or excluded.

The primary purpose of an extent is to provide a candidate collection of objects to be used in a query, where filtering or ordering can be applied.

Nevertheless, it can be used to access all persisted objects of a given class and maybe its subclasses, therefore an *Iterator* is provided by the *Extent* interface.

The data-retrieval process will not start until the first invocation of *next()* on a obtained *Iterator*. Thus, it is possible to delegate an *Extent* to a *Query* without unnecessary data access.

3.6. JDO-Query Language

The aim of the JDO-Query Language is to provide a simple query grammar that is familiar to Java programmers and that can be executed by the JDO implementation, possibly by converting it to a different representation and passing it to the underlying data store. Hence, it abstracts from data store languages like SQL or other datastore depending premises.

JDO enables vendor-specific enhancements and additional query languages. In some implementations it is possible to use SQL query statements concurrent to native JDO-QL queries.

A query itself consists of a set of candidate instances, which can be specified using a Java class, an *Extent*, or a collection and a filter string. In addition it is also possible to declare import statements, parameters and variables as well as an ordering for the set of results. When executed, a query takes the set of candidate instances and returns a Java collection of references to the instances that satisfies the query filter.

Queries will be highly optimized on the underlying datastore, depending on the JDO implementation. For instance, *Extents* can internally be used to produce an equivalent query in native data store language.

Filter strings of JDO-QL can consist of attribute names, logical operators, references on objects and a few methods related to strings or objects.

For instance, a filter string can be 'attrName == \"string\"'. A few common supported logical operators are !, &&, | |, <, >, ==, etc. Indeed, for string comparison no SQL like *like*-operator is supported. JDO provides *startsWith()* and *endsWith()* constraints. To assists work with collections of objects, *isEmpty()* and *contains(Object o)* are specified.

In comparison with SQL or other common query languages JDO-QL is limited to the very basics in version 1.0.1, but will be enhanced in the upcoming JDO 2.0 standard.

4. Outlook on JDO 2.0

The upcoming revision of JDO, so called JDO 2.0, is finally approved. It will provide several improvements to the first version of Java Data Objects.

In particular, JDO 2.0 implementations will be binary compatible to all earlier versions and among each other. Nevertheless, it will introduce new interesting additional features.

One of the main targets had been to specify a standard object/relational mapping to improve JDO's acceptance among the general programming public. Standardized mapping and runtime behavior will improve portability between different JDO implementations and will increase utility of vendor independent tools.[2]

Furthermore, JDO 2.0 will introduce an attach/detach API, which will simplify handling objects in multi-tier applications. For instance, an application has to transfer an object to a client and allow the client to modify its states. Afterwards, the object has to be returned and the modifications done have to be saved.

Maybe, the most important improvements had been done on the JDO-Query Language. Its capabilities had been enhanced a lot, compared to JDO 1.0. The JDO-QL will now support aggregates, named queries, projections and additional functions for string-related and mathematic operations.

In JDO 1.0 all query results had been a collection of objects identified by the query. Since addition of projections and aggregates in JDO 2.0 a result can be an array of objects, which represents a table of records with named columns.

The newly supported aggregate functions are *count()*, *sum()*, *avg()*, *min()*, and *max()*. The following functions had been introduced to enhance string and math capabilities:

- *get(Object)* applies to Map types
- *containsKey(Object)* applies to Map types
- *containsValue(Object)* applies to Map types
- *toLowerCase()* applies to String type
- *toUpperCase()* applies to String type
- *indexOf(String)* applies to String type
- *matches(String)* applies to String type, but only the following regular expression patterns are required to be supported: Global "(?i)" for case-insensitive matches; and "." and ".*" for wild card matches.
- *substring(int, int)* applies to String type
- *Math.abs(numeric)*
- *Math.sqrt(numeric)*
- *JDOHelper.getObjectId(Object)* static method in JDOHelper, allows using the object identity of an instance directly in a query.

5. Conclusion

Persistence is one of the most important concepts in business applications. Therefore, an easy to use and common interface is required to meet business requirements.

JDO will meet these requirements in most cases. It is a standardized interface-based definition of object persistence, which is supported by leading vendors.

Provided transparency will help to reduce modeling and programming efforts, compared to ordinary JDBC and SQL usage, which nevertheless is not obsolete in specific use cases. Furthermore, the abstraction of specific data storage will lead to an improved portability of the whole application.

The programmer itself will benefit in an API for accessing persistent data with object model information only and tools which provide this transparency by automated code enhancement.

While JDO 1.0 may not suit anyone, JDO 2.0 will bring a lot of promising improvements and may be considered when choosing a persistence framework.

References

[JDOSPEC] Java Data Objects Specification
http://jcp.org/aboutJava/communityprocess/final/jsr012/index2.html

[JDO20DRAFT] Java Data Objects 2.0 Public Draft
http://jcp.org/aboutJava/communityprocess/pr/jsr243/index2.html

[FMC] Fundamental Modeling Concepts
http://www.f-m-c.org/notation-reference/

[JDOC] JDO Java Doc
http://java.sun.com/products/jdo/javadocs/

[UUJDO2003] David Ezzio,
Using and Understanding Java Data Objects, Apress, 2003

[JDOPH2003] Sameer Tyagi et al.
Core Java Data Objects, Prentice Hall PTR, 2003

[JDOAW2003] Robin M. Roos,
Java Data Objects, Addison Wesley, 2003

[JDOO2003] David Jordan and Craig Russell,
Java Data Objects, O'Reilly, 2003

[HOLU2004] Andreas Holubek,
Java Data Objects in der Praxis,
Javamagazin 06/2004

---

[2] E.g. Versant offers an Eclipse plug-in for JDO based development as open source software http://www.versant.com/opensource/orm/en-us

YOUR KNOWLEDGE HAS VALUE

- We will publish your bachelor's and
  master's thesis, essays and papers

- Your own eBook and book -
  sold worldwide in all relevant shops

- Earn money with each sale

Upload your text at www.GRIN.com
and publish for free